Changes in Childbirth

Changes in Childbirth

Researched & written
by Deborah Durbin

COUNTRY BOOKS

Published by: Country Books
Courtyard Cottage, Little Longstone, Bakewell, Derbyshire DE45 1NN

ISBN 1 898941 28 9

British Library Cataloguing in Publication Data:
a catalogue record for this book is available from the British Library.

Design and production by:
Dick Richardson, Country Books, Little Longstone, Derbyshire DE45 1NN

Printed in England by:
MFP Design & Print, Stretford, Manchester M32 0JT

Origination by:
GA Graphics, Stamford, Lincolnshire PE9 2RB

Acknowledgements
Why changes in childbirth?

I never had a reason to concern myself with motherhood or child-birth until I became a parent myself in 1993 with my daughter Rebecca. It was only when I found myself chatting to other mothers who already had children, that I discovered just how much our practices and attitudes with regard to childbirth and motherhood had changed over the years.

As a working journalist and writer, my first though was that this subject would make a good feature for one of the many parenting magazines on the market and I contacted Debbie Thrower of BBC Radio Two, who kindly announced that I was looking for mothers to contribute their stories of their own experiences of childbirth for the research for such an article.

Well, what a surprise I got! I was overwhelmed with letters from all over the country and found that, not only did I have more than enough information to actually compile a book about how practices in childbirth had changed, but also that it was a subject that is very dear to women and one which they wanted to hear about. And so Changes in Childbirth was born, so to speak.

All children are uniquely special and despite the fact that millions of women in the world experience childbirth everyday, each and every experience is also unique and special and I would like to take this opportunity to thank all the women who wrote to me and allowed me to share their experiences on this fascinating subject and also to thank Debbie Thrower of BBC Radio Two, for airing the subject in the first place.

I would also like to thank my husband Richard for his patience while I tapped away for hours on end on the PC and his tolerance when I read and re-read chapters out to him. I thank my sister Helen for all her advice and inspiration when it seemed as though I was going around in circles for evermore. My thanks also to Weston General Hospital where my first daughter was born and to St. Michael's Hospital in Bristol where my second daughter was born. Thank you to my publisher Dick Richardson for all his help. And of course I thank my two beautiful daughters, Rebecca and Georgina — two of the greatest gifts of my life, who without them, this book would never have been written.

Foreword

Frightening. Wonderful. Overwhelming. Scary. Anxious Euphoric. Mind-blowing — These are just some of the feelings women have described about their experiences of giving birth to their children. Just as women's experiences differ, so too have our attitudes and practices towards childbirth as a nation, which have changed dramatically over the past fifty years.

The 1940's and 1950's showed us that home births were often the norm and maternity services were to be paid for prior to the birth. Father's-to-be were not allowed near a delivery room and visits were kept to a strict minimum. Even as late as the 60's, single mothers were often treated as if they were second class citizens and not just by the general public, but also by the maternity staff and many times the only pain relief available was to bite on a rolled up towel.

How times have changed! Thankfully today we see the latest in medical technology and now we are fortunate enough to have one of the best maternity care services in the world. More and more women are choosing elective caesareans — something that was almost unheard of thirty years ago and with the introduction of Epidurals and harmless pain killing drugs, the future now ensures that women can have a pain free and enjoyable labour and child birth.

CHANGES IN CHILDBIRTH takes a look at the changes that have taken place over the years in women's experiences of childbirth and maternity care with a compilation of thirty true stories as told, in their own words, by the women who experienced them.

Many of the stories from women all over the country, aged between 18 to 85 will astound and amaze you.

Many will make you laugh, like when Irene defiantly locked herself in the toilet until the hospital staff would listen to her requests. Others will make you cry, like when Ellen gave birth to a stillborn baby and was transferred to a ward full of nursing mothers and their babies for six weeks.

Read their own stories about the most important role in a

woman's life, in this interesting and heart-warming account of the history of childbirth from the 1940's to the 1990's.

* Some names have been changed to protect identity and all contributors have given their permission to have their story published.

* * * *

About the author

Deborah Durbin qualified as a journalist three years ago and since then has worked as a successful freelance journalist for women's magazines, parenting magazines and newspapers. She has also written a novel and a screen play for TV and is the editor of a local paper. She and her husband Richard live in a small village in North Somerset and together they have two daughters, Rebecca five and Georgina two.

Deborah juggles her successful career in writing with motherhood; which she describes as the hardest but most rewarding job she's ever done. This is her first non-fiction book.

**"I CREATED YOU SO THAT YOU CAN CREATE THE WORLD
AND ALL THAT IS ON THE WORLD"**

(Hindu Mythology & Philosophy)

*This book is dedicated to my Mum & Dad,
who created me, cared for me
and believed in me — Thanks Mum, Thanks Dad.*

CONTENTS

CHAPTER ONE
1940's

It was often tough for women expecting babies in the 1940's. With little help from the NHS, the majority of women had to pay for any maternity care prior to having their babies, which often cost almost an average weekly wage.

The attitudes of nursing and midwifery staff were often hostile and frightening and according to at least one story, the sterilising of equipment was something of an afterthought.

On no circumstances did fathers attend their children's births and women were often left alone for long periods of time. Some women were even told to 'Shut-Up!' if they requested assistance from a nurse during their labour.

Read Ella's story, when upon being told that her baby was in the breech position, was also told to grit her teeth and get on with it. Patricia was told that she had another month to go, only to give birth that very day and on her own and Eileen had four very different childbirth experiences — before, during and after the war ...

Eileen's Story

Eileen, now 85, has four children. The first was born in 1937 before the war; the second in 1942 during the war and the following two children after the war. Here is her story . . .

"I had my first daughter, who is now sixty years old, at home in 1937. In those days you generally had a home birth if everything was fine with your pregnancy and there was never a lot of fuss over an expectant mother back then — It was just the done thing, you got married and had children.

I had a midwife in attendance who was staying with us for the few days prior to the birth. We were all sitting down for tea when my labour pains started and this efficient midwife suddenly rushed me upstairs and told me to lie down on the bed immediately. As the pains progressed, she decided to call for the doctor. When he arrived he told me that I would need an anaesthetic. This was administered by dropping drips into a cone of paper, which was placed over my nose and mouth — I don't remember anything after that!

When I did recover, I awoke to find that the bottom of my bed had been ripped up — I guess they had run out of swabs! My husband must have wondered what on earth was going on upstairs! I had a beautiful baby girl who was just fine and I was ordered to rest for two weeks as I had lost a lot of blood during the delivery.

I remember being very down in the mouth — the baby-blues, I think they call it now a days, but my mother came to stay with us which helped me immensely.

When I had my second child Christopher, the war was on and by then we had moved to Surrey — this being my father's idea that they would never be able to bomb London (Ha, Ha!) I had a very young doctor for this birth who was very efficient, but I was told that I was going to be too late to be admitted to the new maternity ward, which was being built in the near-by hospital, so I went to stay as a patient to the maternity nurses own home.

The nurse only took one patient at a time, so I dread to think what would happen if we'd had a baby boom! I enjoyed myself immensely; it was like being at a hotel. My birth started at around 1.15 in the morning after I ate an apple and had just had my dose of Castor Oil — a revolting solution that was given to all mothers-to-be whose babies were due.

By 6.30 the same morning Christopher was born and with no painkillers at all! Everything went very well indeed and the nurse and doctor both stayed by my bedside and chatted to me after I'd been cleaned up. This was by far the best experience I had with all of my children, although my husband was away in France at the time, so I was pretty much alone and didn't get to see him for a long time.

My third birth was with my daughter Louise and was the most miserable time of all and the most annoying. My husband had been de-mobbed and thought that I deserved a bit of luxury, so he booked me into the most expensive nursing home he could find — big mistake!

When we arrived, I was in a lot of pain and we were told that we should have come earlier. I just wanted to turn around and go back out of the door. I would have rather had my baby on my own.

I was taken into a room with just a bed in it and the door was left wide open for all and sundry to see what was going on. At one point I could hear another patient groaning in pain and pleading for help and I thought I'm not going to like this one little bit. There was certainly no room for tea and sympathy in that nursing home! I desperately wanted to go to the loo and I managed to get to the bathroom by myself, but as I climbed back into bed, my waters broke and I began to shout for help.

After about five minutes, a nurse strolled in and told me quite abruptly that a doctor would over-see my birth and give me painkillers, then she went again. Unfortunately, the doctor didn't arrive until my daughter Louise was born! He did apologise for not being there, but apparently the nurses had forgotten to call him until it was too late and I didn't get my painkillers either! I managed without them. It was sharp and short and over quite quickly, Thank goodness!

I left that place as soon as I could and was furious when, returning home I spoke to my friends who all said that they knew that it was an awful home but didn't like to tell me!

When I had my fourth and final child, I decided to stay at home. I'd had enough of being pulled and poked about by strangers and felt more than experienced to handle the situation myself. My labour pains started at about nine in the morning and went on all day. The District nurse called in two or three times and by midnight I was bent double with the pains and wondered if I should have gone to the hospital rather than stay at home.

The procedure with the anaesthetic was still the same as when I had my first child, only this time I was able to administer the anaesthetic myself during the birth and I felt that I had more control over it — maybe because I was older and wiser this time around! At around midnight, a very squally baby arrived and this time I stood no nonsense. I lugged him into bed with me and we both slept right through the night!

All my four children were breast-fed from birth until they were six months old. I followed Doctor Truby King's strict regime and put them straight onto full cow's milk after the initial six months — fed in a cup. It was a struggle at first, but they all soon got use to it, so I never had the need for a babies bottle!"

Phyllis's Story

ONE MONTH TO GO!

Phyllis is now 89, but remembers the birth of her second child in March 1943 quite vividly . . .

"I had just been to the clinic in Bristol for a check up. It was a small and unfriendly place and I didn't know of anyone who liked going there. Upon being examined, the midwife told me that I had at least another month to go, but I felt so bloated and fat, just to walk was a struggle, that I was sure she was wrong.

I went home feeling fed up and tired but did all the usual day to day chores, despite it being a struggle to get up and down the stairs! I'd had an uneasy feeling that all was not well for a few days and was very restless throughout the night.

That night I couldn't sleep and had to get up to spend a penny every five minutes. My husband was in the National Fire Service, but was with me at home that night and at about four o'clock in the morning I awoke to find that I was in labour and I told my husband to go and fetch the midwife immediately.

We didn't have a phone or a car and it was quite a long walk to her house and she certainly didn't rejoice at having my husband hammering on her door in the early hours of the morning, particularly when she had told me that very day that I had another four weeks to go!

My baby wanted to get out as quickly as possible and I had five really bad pains and then my son arrived — before my husband returned with the midwife. I was quite frightened because I was alone in the house, except for my three year old, who was sound asleep in bed. I didn't really know anything about cutting the cord or what I should do next and so just lay there cradling my baby and praying that they would return soon!

Fortunately all turned out well, but what a shock I got when I first heard the baby cry! I never did get an apology from the midwife, who said that my baby must have decided to come early!"

Ella's Story

WE HAD TO BE TOUGH IN THOSE DAYS!

Ella had her first baby in November 1945 and when she was told that he was in the breech position, she knew that she was going to have a hard time . . .

"I was twenty one when I had my son — a breech presentation and the birth is something that I will never forget! I had been informed previously that my baby was lying breech and a specialist tried to turn him, but was unable to. They told me that it was going to be a difficult birth and that any danger would possibly be to the baby. Naturally I was more than a little apprehensive!

I had booked myself into a private nursing home so that I could be near to my family for visits. My husband was an Officer in the Merchant Navy and was somewhere in Australia at the time, so I was very much alone. There was no mention of a caesarean for me, as I believe is the option now-a-days.

As soon as my water's broke, I was rushed into the hospital by a taxi, which a friend had ordered for me. I was then taken into the delivery room that held a bed and a small cot — just the basics! The pains were very strong and sharp and I was left all on my own and told that I should walk around and find something to grab hold of when the pains got more intense — there was no mention of pain relief! The pains were coming every half a minute and I was more or less confined to gripping the end of the metal bed.

A nurse popped her head around the door and said "Do be a good girl and try not to ring the bell, we're ever so busy dear!" Then she went again. Sometime during the evening I was brought a glass of milk and after that I didn't see anyone until I screamed the place down that I wanted to push.

The same nurse called for my doctor when three hours of pushing and hard work (now I know why they call it labour) seemed endless and a few minutes before the birth the doctor clapped a mask over my face and told me to breath in and out. This was apparently 'Ether', but had I not been a private patient and had my own doctor in attendance, I doubt very much that I would have been given it.

I was hanging over the side of the bed with a young nurse holding my feet to help me push and the Sister holding on to my shoulders so that I wouldn't fall off the other end!

It took a while before I heard my baby cry and he was briefly held up for me to see and then whisked away for Oxygen as he was struggling to breathe.

I didn't see my baby again for fifteen hours, that following evening. I didn't know why. I never did get an explanation and was naturally worried that something had happened to him. I expect he was distressed with being so long in the birth channel which of course is monitored these days.

We certainly had to be tough in those days, but I think the feeling of achievement was far greater than it is today — after all, no pain relief, no monitors, scans or pain killers, it was certainly an achievement! But what a beautiful baby I had and all at the age of twenty one!"

Betty's Story

FATHER'S WERE KEPT
WELL OUT OF THE PICTURE!

Betty had her children in 1946 and 1948, when, she says, very little information was available for mothers to be . . .

"My first experience of childbirth I feel was done in the old fashioned way, and the second was much more modern — for those days anyway, although prehistoric compared to now-a-days!

On the first occasion, I knew very little of what to expect and had been told that a normal delivery would not be possible due to previous medical history. I was admitted to a labour ward when I could bear the pains no longer and I was in fact well advanced in labour. After being 'prepped' by an almost silent nurse, I was left on my own for some considerable amount of time.

A while later, I was told to use the gas and air machine if I needed it and was eventually supervised until I produced a normal healthy baby, but everything was so formal and unfriendly. I had no one to hold my hand like they do today and the nursing staff just didn't seem interested at all. The only comment I did get was from the doctor who stitched me up, thanking me for a speedy delivery!

Before my next pregnancy, I prepared myself by reading Doctor Grantly Dick Read's book, *Natural Childbirth*. This book was the only one about childbirth at the time and then only available from the library, under the counter. I also watched a film at a Bristol cinema about a normal delivery and felt better prepared than the first time around and actually quite excited that this time, I would know just what was going on and would be more in control.

I taught myself relaxation and how to breathe properly — which the staff thought most odd! But I felt ready and happy to go through it all this time. I was very lucky with both of my births because they were so quick and the second time around I felt that I was able to help myself more, although the attitude of the staff had not changed, which I believe may have accounted for a second tear.

I stayed in hospital for twelve days for my first baby and ten for my second. Back then babies were fed at three-hour intervals, except during the night, irrespective of their birth weight and this resulted in my first baby being over-fed. I believe that this still often happens today and babies are all treated the same with regards to their feeds.

My post-natal period in hospital was trying! The only time we saw our babies was when it was time for a feed. The rest of the time they were placed into the nursery, so you had no idea what was happening to them. The staff were all very serious and I often wondered why they were in the 'caring' profession at all! It was only when you got home that you felt that you were allowed really to get to know your baby, before then you were just required to feed your baby and hand him back.

Fathers were kept well out of the picture and were certainly not allowed into the nursery. They were only allowed into the lying in wards during the evenings for half an hour. My husband was allowed to see our baby during this visit, but only through a glass window and other family members had to wait until the mother came out of hospital

It was portrayed that the mothers needed time to recover, but really we needed to be with our loved ones and allowed to bond with our babies.

I am envious of today's mothers and the more understanding approach generally to childbirth, especially the trend to having babies and then being allowed home a few hours afterwards, there was never a question of it back then!"

Connie's Story

I WAS TOLD THAT HE WOULDN'T LAST THE NIGHT!

Connie is now 75 years old, but still remembers her experience of childbirth with her first child with a shudder . . .

"My first baby, a little boy, was born in October 1946. He is now 53 years old and with children of his own, but at the time we didn't know if he would make it through his first night!

I was in labour with him for three whole days and in a very bad way. In those days it was quite rare to get help through the NHS and the majority of people had to pay for their maternity care. The hospital I attended was a former workhouse and cost me and my husband seven pounds, a lot of money back then considering that my husband only earned five pounds a week! A private maternity home would have cost twenty pounds a week plus a fee for you own doctor. Everything seemed to be a great inconvenience back then when you were expecting a baby.

We were not informed about sex education at school and if you hadn't been told about the facts of life from your mother, you would simply pick them up from friends who had. It was normal then for a girl to leave school, maybe work for a short time and then get married and start a family and it was thought very odd if a girl wasn't married by the time she was twenty three! — How times have changed, women today often don't settle down until their well into their 30's.

It was also very scary for young women back then, but you never admitted it and never asked questions, even if you didn't have a clue about what was going on! Our mothers never did and their mothers never did. It was really a case of just getting on with it.

I had no help from the maternity home that I was admitted to and was very frightened about the whole thing. I didn't know what was going on with my own body and I remember it all so clearly, but then you tend to remember awful things don't you.

When I had my son, I remember that the ward was full of ants crawling everywhere and I just wanted to get out of there, everywhere I looked there were blooming ants! The only help I received throughout my whole painful labour was when a midwife smacked my bottom to stop me screaming!

When my son was born he was held upside down by his feet and shaken violently like a dead rabbit. He was whisked away, before I had the chance to see him and I was told simply 'Sorry, your baby's very ill and he won't last the night!'

What a thing to say!

I found out later that my son had Septicaemia of the umbilicus and he was given brandy and water to try and help him. When I was allowed to see him, he smelt terrible and was panting for breath all the time. I couldn't bear to see him struggling and it broke my heart. There was my little baby boy struggling for life and I couldn't do a thing to help him.

My own father was a doctor at the time and I am sure that if he hadn't turned up, they would have just let my baby die. Doctor's were looked up to like Gods in the old days and in his time and my father had attended everything from a nose bleed to brain surgery.

However, it wasn't correct for him to interfere and he had to be very careful with his words to the maternity home. He had remembered my brothers birth who had been delivered by a very old doctor, who slipped with the forceps whilst trying to deliver him. This caused him to have brain damage and suffer epileptic fits for the rest of his life. My father had seen his son's life turned upside down and was damn sure that he was going to help his grandson as much as he could — he promised me that he wouldn't let him die.

I cried a lot that night, thinking that my baby could be dead by the morning and I would never get to hold him. I didn't get any sympathy from the home, it was a case of 'Well these things happen, I'm afraid.'

Thankfully, my father lived up to his promise and my son survived. That wasn't the end of it though. During my stay I had an infection in my breasts and the midwife who cut the dressing from me, then proceeded to remove the stitches from the lady in the next bed, with the same pair of scissors!

We were both livid, but too afraid to say anything to her at the time, for fear of being told off!

Eight years later, I decided to have another baby and this time it was a little girl. Being the fifties, things were improving slightly, with more care being taken towards the help in childbirth. My daughter was the perfect birth, although I dreaded it at the time due to what had happened to my son.

We were then blessed with another girl, this time a little more difficult because the cord had wrapped itself around her neck and due to a lot of struggling I tore inside, but again she was a healthy baby.

My eldest daughter is now a Sister Midwife and says that she can't believe the way that I was treated when I had my own children. Thankfully today things have improved. I think it must be heaven to have all the wonderful care that there is today — I wish we had it back then!"

Ellen's Story

MY BABY WAS STILL BORN

Ellen found the hospital that she had her baby in to be very unsympathetic at the loss of her baby . . .

"I was pregnant with my first child in 1947 and on January 1st I had an appointment to attend an ante-natal class at the hospital. I was told that my baby was in the breech position and a couple of nurses tried to turn him without success. I was then given another appointment for two weeks later. Still no success and I was told 'Never mind dear, it's a small baby, you'll cope.'

I had a few more appointments and still there was no change, then all of a sudden when I was at home, my water's broke. I rang for an ambulance and was admitted to what was known as a 'Cottage Hospital' — a converted house where most of the local births took place.

When I rang for help, a couple of nurses and several students appeared which I thought was rather odd, but really I just wanted it all over with. I went through some of the most agonising pains and a doctor appeared on the scene and put me to sleep. The last thing I remember seeing was a bright light with chromium tiles around it.

When I awoke momentarily, I saw a little cot being wheeled out of the room, but I wasn't allowed to remain conscious and was told that I shouldn't be awake. I was then given another dose of whatever knocked me out in the first place.

When I was finally allowed to regain consciousness, I was told that my 'small baby' had been born stillborn and he had actually weighed eight and a half pounds!

I couldn't quite believe what I was hearing. One minute I was having a baby and the next I had no baby! I was then subjected to a very painful stitch-up. I think they thought that as it was all over with, they could do what they liked with me and proceeded to stitch me up with no anaesthetic.

I was then put into a bed and wheeled down to a totally dark corridor and left alone in a bewildered and thirsty state.

As dawn broke, someone brought me a tepid cup of tea and my husband arrived at about eight that morning. A few hours later I was transferred to a ward where a dozen or so new mothers were busy breast feeding their babies!

The only thing anyone said to me was that my bladder had been displaced and that I was to drink plenty of water. I was left in this ward and milk was coming out of my breasts and I had no baby to feed and hold.

I had to stay in that same ward, watching mother's come and go, for six weeks — how insensitive can you get. I couldn't grieve for my child that I had lost and I was devastated. During this time my husband went to the cemetery to see our son buried — in a paupers grave. It was the worse time of my life and I will never forget it.

Thankfully, two years later, I had another baby who was a healthy, beautiful and content little thing — a real joy, but I will never forget my first baby — not ever."

CHAPTER TWO
1950's

Conditions in childbirth and maternity care had still not improved much ten years later. Pain relief was limited and women were warned that if they intended to have a baby, then they must expect a lot of pain and a long, hard labour.

Again, the NHS did not help anymore than they did in the 40's and a lot of women relied heavily on the maternity hospitals which were run by The Salvation Army, which cost about seven pounds. Other than that, the only other option for women was to pay for a private hospital, which cost a lot more.

Maternity care was still likened by some to being in the army and information about childbirth was not readily available. The recovery time spent in hospital was usually two weeks and women were strictly confined to bed rest for that period.

Women who'd had a successful birth were expected to have any additional children at home and home delivery maternity staff were coming around to a more positive attitude towards mothers to be.

Read how, when Mary Louise finally gave birth to a son, she was paid five pounds and how Doreen suffered at the hands of a 'smack-happy' midwife! . . .

Mary-Louise's Story

I WAS PAID FIVE POUNDS
FOR HAVING MY SON!

Mary Louise had her first child, a girl in 1950. Another daughter followed before she finally gave birth to a much-wanted boy. She was paid five pounds for having him ...

"My first child Anne was born early at eight months and weighed only 4lb 5oz, very tiny and considered quite dangerous. When I had given birth to her — in a panic because I knew that she was going to be under weight, she was rushed away and put into an incubator. I was told that I couldn't see her because she was so poorly, she had jaundice and I was informed that it would be at least a week, before I could see my daughter again and give her a cuddle. That time was agonising. I couldn't let her know that I was there for her and so just had to sit and wait.

When I did get to see her, she was very orange in colour, as if she had a sun tan and they tried to get her to latch on to me for a feed, but she just refused to take any milk. This was also heart breaking because all I wanted was to make everything better for her. In the end the hospital tried every kind of milk available every three hours to find out what type she would accept.

I was in hospital for a month with my daughter and then I was allowed to go home, but in that month it seemed as if time had stood still. I was elated when I was told that we could go home and my daughter came home weighing just five pounds.

I still had to visit the hospital once a fortnight for her check-ups and to make sure that she was still eating properly. I was told that she wasn't allowed on public transport because of the risk of infection to her and so I had to walk to the hospital every two weeks , which was quite a way.

The staff were quite abrupt in those days, but I had other things on my mind and I just ignored them most of the time! Today my daughter is 48 years old and with children of her

27

own, but I still worry about her!

My second pregnancy went well throughout, although she was early too, by ten days. Then came our little boy! I wondered if I would ever have a boy and this was the most pleasurable experience of them all. I was told that as I didn't have any problems with my previous children's births, I should have this one at home and save on resources!

I had a midwife booked and she was very good at her job, telling me when to stop pushing, which was quite difficult, but he was born in two and a half hours! Later the midwife told me that I was lucky to have him, because the umbilical cord had twisted twice around his neck when he was delivered.

My poor husband was frantic with worry downstairs when I had our son, but at last I had a boy to carry on the family name! It was such a big occasion and my father-in-law was so pleased with his grandson that he gave me five pounds, which was a lot of money in those days. I remember he folded up the note in my hand and said with a smile, 'You go out and treat yourself my dear, well done'.

I feel that I was very lucky to have three wonderful babies who have proved a great comfort to me, especially now that my husband has passed on. I am left with children who look after and do what they can for me. I never regretted one moment of it all — The best feeling in the world!"

Doreen's Story

I HAD MY LEGS SMACKED BY THE MIDWIFE!

When I was conducting the research for this book, I received a letter from a lady called Doreen, now 75 years of age. She said that she had used a lot of tissues when writing to me . . .

"I was twenty six when I had my first child and had been married for four years. I remember the birth being extremely painful, but that was to be expected — or so I was told! My labour took a day and night, twenty nine hours in total and during that time I was in terrible pain and felt very scared.

I was left alone because husbands were not allowed in the maternity hospital, which at the time was run by the Salvation Army. We had to pay for this service which was about seven pounds, a lot of money back then. To get a maternity hospital run by the NHS was like getting gold and so the majority of people had to pay for any care that they received.

When I called for help, I was told to 'Shut up and go back to sleep!' and also that it would be several hours before I gave birth. As you can imagine, I was terrified.

I was still very young in terms of today's women and I didn't have anyone that I knew with me, just all these strangers yelling at me to be quiet!

When my baby was finally being delivered, the midwife who was assigned to me, kept shouting at me to try harder and then slapped my legs in annoyance at me! I was too frightened to say anything, although I did get an apology later on, but the manner in which I was treated was appalling.

Believe it or not, it didn't put me off though and I became pregnant for the second time three years later. During this pregnancy I was quite ill and I had extremely high blood pressure and was told to rest. With a toddler to care for, this was near impossible and so I carried on as normal. This birth was very quick, just four hours, but so sharp!

I was given adrenaline injections afterwards but I developed

Thrombosis and was ordered to bed for three weeks. I think my poor husband thought my time was up!

I think that now-a-days, a patient with high blood pressure would spend most of their pregnancy in hospital hopefully saving a lot of trouble later on. When I was discharged, I was told that I must have a home help for a couple of weeks — another thing that had to be paid for. Our local council didn't want to know until my husband threatened to withhold our rent. They finally paid for it all!

My third baby was born at home; there was no way that I was going back to that hospital again! I had my very own midwife who gave me the best personal attention and care a woman could ask for. She told me when to stop pushing so that I wouldn't tear and this was the easiest birth of them all.

People think that home births are relatively new, yet most women my age have had at least one of their children at home. It's not a new thing at all; it's just gone full circle.

That was my family complete — or so I thought. At the grand old age of 45, I became pregnant again. I had all the usual symptoms — sickness, tiredness and of course my periods had stopped. When I went to see the doctor, he told me not to be so silly and that my periods had to stop sometime!

Sadly, three months into the pregnancy, I miscarried. The doctor was very unsympathetic and simply said to my husband 'Oh well, at least you know you've still got it in you!' There was no care for me this time, none at all. A couple of days later, I was vacuuming when my daughter called in to see me. She told me to sit down saying that the Doctor had pulled up outside and she thought that he must want to check me over. No such thing! He merely wanted my signature on a form to say that he had attended a miscarriage so that he could be paid for it!

I think these days a D & C is automatically performed after a miscarriage, but I wasn't given one and eventually I had to have a hysterectomy which took a long time to recover from.

When I think back at how I was treated with my childbirth's and pregnancy's I do get angry, but one didn't tend to question them back then. I just hope no other woman is treated like this now a days!

Joan's Story

MY MOTHER WARNED ME
HOW AWFUL IT WAS GOING TO BE!

Joan, 70, recalls being terrified at the prospect of having children after her mother had drummed it into her that it was a pain beyond belief . . .

"I had my first child at the age of 21 and despite my own mother's awful experience with childbirth, I was determined that I was going to have a happy and relaxed time.

My 'Bible' was *The Natural Childbirth* book, which I read over and over again — I was going to be prepared for this birth if nothing else!

My pregnancy was perfect, no morning sickness and because I was having my baby at home — the normal way that deliveries were carried out then, I was allocated a lovely midwife who I got to know really well. She was like a second mother to me — my own mother lived some 150 miles away.

When the day came — a day after my due date, I slept right through the first stages of labour, which must have started sometime during the night and awoke at about six the following morning with the second stages already taking place.

I called my midwife and she stayed with me until nine o'clock when my baby boy was born. It was just as I'd hoped it would be, not much pain and he came out so easily, I even managed to sit up and watch him appear.

I did have quite severe bleeding and the midwife gave me an injection to stop the flow of blood. I also needed a few stitches so she called in our local doctor to attend to this.

He was our new GP and this was his first home delivery, so he took quite a time in stitching me up, or as the midwife put it, 'You could have embroidered a table cloth in the time he took to do that!'

In those days it just wasn't considered that a husband should attend the birth of his child and he just sat and waited and wondered! Our baby was eight and a half pounds and I breast fed him for three months very easily. I enjoyed the experience so much that I said I would have had another tomorrow if I could.

Two years and one month later, our second baby arrived. I was so looking forward to having another problem free pregnancy and childbirth. I was twelve days overdue with this one and I remember that the pains were so intense that I had to eat my dinner from the mantel piece because it was so uncomfortable to sit down!

When my midwife — the same one, arrived she said 'Sorry, Joan, no time for pudding' and whisked me upstairs. She and I were determined that I would not need any stitches this time and she controlled my pushing until out he popped a hefty ten pounds! He was absolutely gorgeous and already looking like a month old baby at birth. I was calling for my pudding soon afterwards!

It certainly was different in those days. If you had your baby at home, you got to know your midwife on a personal basis, not like today when you don't know who you'll be with from one day to the next. When my children were born, you had to stay in bed for a week and were not even allowed to take a warm bath in that week, but the rest was wonderful.

I can honestly say that my experiences were a wonderful and a joyous time. My own mother could not believe how well it all went and I'm sure she thought I was making it up! However, maybe she did have cause to complain. I was born seven weeks premature, weighing under three pounds and landed head first down a chamber pot!"

CHAPTER THREE
1960's

Although things were improving for mothers-to-be who had their children at home, this appears to be the opposite for women having their children in the hospitals.

Single mothers were highly disapproved of, not only in public, but also in the hospitals and if your baby decided to come early, well it was just too bad! Many women have complained that midwives had still not come round to the idea of being 'customer friendly' and women felt unable to ask for the help they needed.

Father's-to-be were still not allowed near the delivery rooms and were often never informed of what was happening to their wives and children. Women were also made to wait to have stitches administered or any other matter of urgency.

Read Rosemary's story of her experience of being a single mother in the sixties and how Nicky's fourth child took six days to actually be delivered!

Ann had a horrific encounter of childbirth with her first child, resulting in her decision not to have another one and Margaret was left on the loo! . . .

Rosemary's Story

I WAS AN 'ORIGINAL' UNMARRIED MOTHER!

Despite a high percentage of unmarried mothers now a days, Rosemary found that being an unmarried mother in the sixties was just not the done thing . . .

"My experience of childbirth in the 60's was a harrowing and disturbing occasion.

I was an unmarried mother in 1961, when a woman in my situation was heavily censured in all quarters. When I went into labour I was first deposited at the North Middlesex Hospital, where the indignities began. There was no information forthcoming about anything concerning my labour. It was decided that the birth was to be normal so, without consultation with me I was transferred to the Maternity Unit in the elegant Bishops Avenue. I found it impossible to get any indication on how long labour might be and was told to just keep walking about.

The day passed and the baby seemed reluctant to make an entrance. The room I shared with another girl was comfortable. The other occupant seemed rather remote and she eventually told me that I was not suitable company. When the labour became more intense I was taken to the Labour Ward and left there entirely alone, looked at occasionally but otherwise left. I was lying on a hard table with one pillow but no covering at all. I was getting colder and colder as the night moved on; I was wearing a gown with a gap down the back. I was shivering with pain and cold but summoning a nurse did nothing to relieve my distress.

I was informed that a woman like me couldn't expect to get any sympathetic treatment and to stop making an unnecessary fuss. There was no pain relief for me — the gas and air machine had no face mask — I struggled to get some relief. Was it deliberate?

At dawn the following morning my daughter was delivered — a truly natural childbirth — not intentional on my part. I was so demoralised and tired out by the experience that I didn't have the guts to complain to the day shift staff. My daughter was well looked after during the two weeks we spent after birth. Later I heard that the Sister, who felt she needed to punish me was dismissed from the N.H.S.

The attitude to illegitimate birth nowadays is so relaxed that it must be a joy to give birth. Even the Grandfather I adored rejected both myself and my daughter. That attitude that was not uncommon was difficult to cope with and so I had to often pretend that I had no child.

Angela's Story

I HAD A WONDERFUL CHILDBIRTH THANKS TO SELF-HELP!

Angela had her children just twenty two months apart, but found the answer to a successful birth the second time around . . .

"My first child Mark is now 35 years old, but his birth was not one that I remember fondly! I had a good pregnancy, with only one check up at six weeks to confirm that I was expecting and then just the occasional blood pressure and urine checks with my local doctor. I think I saw the hospital consultant twice, which again was routine.

We did have four, half hour breathing exercise classes to attend, but all these were with a different teacher and I didn't feel that they helped very much anyway.

When I went into labour, ten days late, I arrived at the hospital about midnight and actually felt quite relaxed and happy at this stage. My husband was not allowed to stay with me, which made me feel rather lost and alone, but otherwise I was fine and looking forward to the birth.

I was told that I must take sleeping tablets but I didn't want to and said so. It was then insisted that I took them and so I did. This was a big mistake as I awoke at five in the morning, in great pain but too sleepy to want to bother about it.

So many midwives came in and out, it was total confusion and one midwife even told me to hurry up because she wanted to get off duty!

I desperately tried to remember my breathing exercises, but every time I tried to start they slapped a mask on my face which made me even drowsier. I couldn't get comfortable and in the end I thought, well the baby has got to be born, so I had better just get on with it!

Eventually after a lot of the necessary grunting and groaning, my wonderful 9lb 5oz son arrived in the world. Pink, plump and adorable and worth all the discomfort, but I had been badly torn and needed many stitches inside.

Later in the day, I couldn't pass urine and I was told that this was normal, but after hours of discomfort, it turned out that I had been stitched too tightly. I had to have a catheter inserted for four days and was on so many antibiotics — I felt awful!

I had to stay in hospital for ten days, which was normal back then and the consultant visited me before I left and said 'My word, what a large baby, when you have another, I think we will give you a caesarean as you are so small boned.'

'Not if I have anything to do with it!' I replied.

Twenty two months later, I had another baby boy — he was late as well. This time I decided to take matters into my own hands and I trained myself in a method of relaxation called Psychoprophylaxis. This was a method of controlling your childbirth by taking the fear out of it all. Unfortunately, I don't think this method is around today, but I wish it were still available for women.

I was taught to be in control right from the start and to control any pain with breathing exercises and muscle relaxation. The basic idea is that quite a lot of labour is related to the emotional reaction to pain and if you learn proper relaxation exercises this vanishes.

Exercises started at four months of pregnancy and classes followed right up to the birth.

When I went into labour this time, I had a few vague pains, but slept soundly until four in the morning. I realised that it was 'my day' and had a warm bath as advised, followed by a light snack. It was so nice not to be frightened about it and I told my husband that it was time to go to the hospital, unless he wanted a new career as a midwife!

Throughout the training, I kept asking myself, how this could possibly work and how I was going to stop the pain that I had experienced the last time. But it did work and I was so relaxed that I didn't really feel any of the painful contractions like I did with my first birth.

Soon after I arrived at the hospital, I went into the second stages of labour and it didn't seem too long before I was told that I could start pushing. Between the pushes I was able to rest back on some pillows and I felt quite comfortable. There was a mirror at the end of the bed and I could see my baby's head slowly appearing.

At the very end, the panting and deep breathing were a great help. I was reminded what to do at the right time. I'm not saying that it was completely painless, but I was in control the whole time and I felt no fear at all.

After about an hour our second son Simon was born at 10lb and 4oz and a very healthy baby — simply wonderful. As he was being born, I could see the scars from the stitching twenty two months previous; they stretched a bit but thankfully didn't split. No gas and air and all perfectly natural!

I am not a brave person and I have always been amazed at how I coped, but I am sure that many women would benefit if only this method were more widely available. I am so pleased that the second birth experience thirty three years ago was good. I had just accepted that my first birth experience was normal and something that had to be endured."

Peggy's Story

CASTOR OIL DID THE TRICK!

Peggy waited and waited for her son to arrive and finally took matters into her own hands . . .

"My last pregnancy was with my son, who is thirty four now and I was in my thirties when he was born. He was born at home, which was usual after the first child and his birth date was given for 2nd February.

As the days went by, there was still no sign of him entering the world and I started to hope that he might arrive on 14th (St. Valentines Day), and then on my birthday which was the 17th!

I then had a few problems with my kidneys and other things and my doctor said that if I didn't have the baby by the following day, I would have to go back to the hospital where my daughter had been born. I didn't like it there one bit and I was adamant that I was not going to return!

That evening, I told my husband that I was going into the kitchen and not to come out there. I hated the taste of Castor Oil, but I held my nose and drank a whole bottle of it straight down.

(This is what mother's-to-be were given to start labour off, combined with orange juice and Epsom salts!)

At 5.30 the following morning, I started to have labour pains and by 6.30 I had progressed further, so I decided to wake my husband. He woke rather startled and asked why I hadn't woken him before. I was quite calm and told him to go and phone the midwife.

In those days we didn't have a car or a phone and the nearest phone box was quite a walk from our house and on to the main road. Fortunately, it didn't take the midwife too long to arrive.

She was a real old-fashioned, matronly midwife and she came rushing up the stairs, muttering away to herself. She took one look at me and said 'I don't think you will have this baby for hours yet, I hope you are not wasting my time, because I have got to get my poodle clipped today!' As much discomfort that I was in, I thought 'Bully for the Bloody Poodle!'

As my labour progressed further, the midwife started to panic. I heard her shout to my husband to take my daughter who was only six, downstairs. It was still early in the morning and she must have wondered what on earth was going on. The midwife then started to tell me to take more gas and air quicker and was very anxious for the baby to be born. Being rather muggy from the gas and air, I didn't grasp the importance of the situation.

Thankfully my son was born by 7.30 that morning. The midwife then told my husband to go and call for the doctor, as I needed a number of stitches. He arrived two hours later, by which time I had fully come round.

The midwife told him that I should have an injection to numb me, but he brushed her request away and proceeded to stitch me up.

I felt every jab of that needle going into me. He stuck the needle in so hard at one point that it snapped in half and he more or less just left me after that. The doctor then said, 'I have broken my best needle trying to stitch you up!' I told him that I would buy him a new one when I went to the shop!

The midwife made my son and me comfortable and I dozed off for a few hours until she returned late in the afternoon. She told me later that my son was very blue when he was born, and that she had fortunately realised that the cord was wrapped around his neck three times.

I have always felt pleased that I took that revolting Castor Oil and that the midwife decided not to go home or my son would have been born stillborn.

My own doctor called in the next day to see me; he was an excellent person and was appalled at the way the stitches had been put in. But I improved slowly and I often smile about the events of my son's birth. By the way I never did find out if the poodle got his haircut!"

Anne's Story

I WAS DISCHARGED BUT STILL HAD THE AFTERBIRTH INSIDE ME!

Anne had suffered three miscarriages during her attempts to have children before she did eventually have a child. When she had her second child, she was discharged with the after-birth inside her . . .

"My first experience of pregnancy was a miscarriage in 1961. I was a good convent educated girl and knew very little about re-production, other than that of a rabbit — We had studied this at school! My friend and I decided that it must be different for humans, we were sweet sixteen — can you imagine it now!

When I started to lose that first baby, I just didn't know what was happening. I ran out to a public pay phone and called my mother. She was in total confusion and told me to get to the doctor. I did — on the bus! He was kind enough, but just told me that nature had to take its course and to ring him if I needed any help.

I spent that night in terror, but nature did takes its course and it was all over by the morning. It was no worse than a bad period pain.

When the same thing happened again six months later, I was told that it happened to a lot of women and I still didn't understand what was going on, so when I was well again, I decided to find out as much as I could about the subject.

I returned to the doctor with my new found knowledge and I asked a lot of questions. He said that if it happened again, I was to keep what I 'passed' and to send it to him at once.

It did happen again and he confirmed that it was an early pregnancy. I have the most vivid memories of fishing this lump of slime and blood out of the toilet and into a pretty ashtray with pink roses on it. I was alone in the house and I wonder how I didn't drown in my own tears.

In 1963, when I was 'late' again, I went to the doctors straight away. He said that he could find out at once by sending samples to Leeds Royal Infirmary. The tests came back negative, but eight months later our first baby was born!

I'd had mini-periods all the way through but no one seemed to think this important and I was in bed for four weeks prior to the birth with high blood pressure and when I was two weeks late, I was taken into the hospital and induced. At no time did anyone explain what was happening and why.

I was put onto a drip and my waters were broken. I had to take tablets, but what they were for and why, I don't know.

Thirty six hours later my baby was born and I was put onto Morphine and just remember a lot of pain and confusion. For a long time I was left in the corridor on a trolley and I can only imagine that they were very busy!

After twenty odd external stitches and lord knows how many internal ones I could finally rest. My husband saw his son through a window and I didn't really see him for two whole days. I remember crying a lot and being on my own a lot, my head full of questions and no one to answer them.

The next time I became pregnant, I had hormone injections every two weeks. I've never heard of anyone else who has had them and never knew why I did. This was in 1964 and my baby was a successful and normal delivery. Until that is, my doctor discovered that I had been discharged but still had most of the afterbirth inside of me! This was very un-pleasant and I believe can be dangerous. In the end I had to have a D & C to make sure that it had all gone.

I had another miscarriage two years later, but by this time I knew the routine. However in 1970, I became pregnant again!

My own doctor wouldn't examine me as he said that it might upset things and the baby was fourteen weeks before he would confirm that everything was fine.

After taking dose of anti-biotics to clear up the flu that I was suffering, my baby reacted and four hours later my daughter was born. I remember my husband driving me to the hospital, horn blaring and lights flashing!

I think you will agree, three very different births, but all with some trauma! At no time was I informed about breast-feeding and when I was discharged from hospital, I had no idea how I was going to feed my first baby. We had to go to a neighbour's house who we didn't even know, but I knew that they had a young baby and I asked them if we could borrow some milk!

I am so glad that it is different for women today. I feel we sixties mums will help our daughters more. They are better informed now, what with television and magazines available — it's just a shame that we weren't — but it makes a good story!"

Nicky's Story

SIX DAYS TO DELIVER MY SON!

Nicky says that when she was expecting her fourth child at the age of 36, she was considered to be an older mother. When she was induced to deliver her baby, it actually took six days for him to arrive ...

"I was expecting my fourth child in August 1969 and at the age of thirty six, I was considered to be quite old for having children and because I was having problems with high blood pressure, it was decided two weeks before my baby was due to induce the birth.

I was admitted to the hospital on Wednesday 12th August and immediately put onto a drip. During the first few days, in spite of having quite severe false labour pains and going through eight bottles of whatever was being pumped into my veins, the baby was no nearer to being delivered.

Having already had three children, I knew what to expect and couldn't understand why this one just wasn't coming out!

My arms were both swollen and heavily bandaged from my wrists to my elbows as the fluid leaked into the surrounding tissue and the nurses were now having trouble trying to find a suitable vein in which to place further needles.

On 16th August, I was feeling completely exhausted and the doctor on duty decided to break my waters, assuring me that I would deliver by that evening. As it was, after a horrendously painful labour, my baby son wasn't actually born until 19th August — six days after the original inducement and three days after my waters had been broken!

My baby weighed 6lb 11oz and was quite poorly with it all. He had to be put into an ICU for a couple of days until he was well enough to come home with me.

It is only recently that I have become aware that during the three days after my waters had been broken and up to the time that I finally gave birth, my baby was as risk of infection, because he had nothing around him to protect him!

However, I am pleased to say that apart from a slight heart murmur, he is now a fine healthy, young man of thirty. I sometimes wonder whether the events leading up to his birth could have some bearing on his heart murmur?

After having had three previous normal deliveries, I will never forget the pain and discomfort of this last one. Discussing it with a friend who is a midwife, she assures me that this would not happen now a days — Thank God!"

Ann's Story

I REALLY WENT TO HELL AND BACK!

Ann had her first (and last) child in July 1969. Her experience of childbirth was simply awful for her, hence the reason why she decided not to have anymore children . . .

"In those days the family doctor was allocated so many beds in a local maternity hospital and my GP duly booked me in for July. Because I was solely his patient, all my check ups were with him and I didn't get to meet a midwife, or attend one antenatal class.

I had a trouble free pregnancy and never felt so good, but it did bother me that I didn't know what to expect or of any procedure in the delivery of my baby.

Two weeks before he was born, my waters broke and panicking I rang the doctor who said that I couldn't go to hospital because my bed wasn't booked until July! As I didn't have any pains he told me to just carry on as normal and that the baby would only come when it was ready to. So that's what I did, carried on as normal, but the weight of the baby made me feel as if I had been kicked all over!

I finally went into labour on 4th July and I duly showered and dressed and at six in the morning I woke my husband, who simply told me that he had to go to work!

At eight I phoned my doctor, gave him the details and the duration of the pains and he told me to wait until two that afternoon before ringing the hospital.

Eventually an ambulance was sent for me and the ambulance man was a little worried because he said that he was only trained to attend accidents and not deliveries!

When I got to the hospital, I had to have another shower and the nursing sister came to examine me. She said that the baby would not be born until the next day. By 10.30 that night, I began retching and felt as though I was going to be sick, so I rang the bell for the nurse. The Sister came in and shouted at me for making a fuss. She told me to sit up, but I still felt sick and when she finally examined me, she found that the baby's head was there!

She quickly thrust a mask onto my face and shouted, 'Breathe in this, until I'm ready!' My son was born at 11.15pm, but was taken away from me before I had the chance to see him. The Sister just sat and chatted to another nurse about when she delivered babies in the Congo — I wished she were still there, anywhere except near me!

The placenta refused to leave my body and I asked if they could ring my doctor. I was told that it wasn't necessary. My doctor did arrive later on and said that, had he been given all the facts he would have been able to arrange for his partner, the anaesthetist to help me, but it was too late and that he was sorry but this was going to hurt!

I then was trussed up like a turkey and the Sister told me to hold her hands — she knew that this was going to be unpleasant. I screamed like I had never known before and I gripped that Sister's hands, wishing that it was her neck!

The doctor had to put his arm inside me right up to his elbow to release the placenta and this was all done without any painkillers!

When it was all over, I was given an injection to stop me haemorrhaging and left on a trolley until the next morning. I saw my baby and he was beautiful, but slightly undernourished and only weighed 5lb 2ozs.

My doctor told my parents that I'd had a bad time with it all and that it had hurt him doing it as much as it had hurt me — I don't think so!

The Sister was off work for two days because of the severe bruising that I had given her — tee-hee. I was so glad to be home and no way would I volunteer to go through that again!

The good thing that came out of it was my son. He is head and shoulders above me now and very muscular, but I'm glad that I didn't see that Sister again!

NOTE: *When Ann wrote to me, she apologised about her handwriting because she was shaking from remembering the experience. She said that she had never told anyone this story before in any detail and maybe that's why she felt so upset, she had buried it to the back of her mind for 30 years.*

Margaret's Story

'I WAS LEFT ON THE LOO
AND THE MIDWIFE WENT HOME!'

Margaret, now 55, said that she was terrified of going to hospital alone . . .

"I was only twenty two years old when I had my first baby — the average age for your first child, but rather young by today's figures. I was very nervous about the whole thing. I wanted a child so much, yet young women were not at all educated back then, not like they are nowadays. A young woman simply got married and had a family, that was most women's ambitions. Work was simply seen as a necessity, not as a career as it is today and it was very rare to see a young, married woman working.

My pregnancy was normal — I think. I didn't really know what was suppose to happen and only went to the hospital when my water's broke — I was told that this was the sign to go. When I arrived with my husband at about 8.30 in the evening, the midwife who answered the bell was very grumpy with us. She briskly pulled the arm of my coat and told my husband to leave my bags and say goodbye in the corridor. I remember begging him to stay with me and crying inconsolably. I was told, in no uncertain words, that it was against the rules. My husband put on a brave face and turned and walked away, with me screaming after him to stay. I cried and cried like I had never cried before, the time I needed him most and he wasn't allowed to be with me.

The same midwife put me into a room and gave me an enema without saying a word to me. She looked at my tear stained face and just rolled her eyes to the ceiling. I was in a lot of pain by this time and desperate for the loo, so she dumped me on the toilet with a thump and left me there.

I sat in that bathroom for what seemed like ages and as I tried to get up, I realised that I couldn't make it on my own. I was so nervous and in so much pain that I didn't know what to do with myself.

After what seemed like an eternity, I nervously called for help. My calls echoed through the quiet hospital unanswered and the more I called, the more I realised that I may well end up having my baby down the toilet!

Eventually, two midwives heard my cries, purely by chance as they walked past the bathroom. They didn't even know that anyone was in there until they heard me crying. Apparently, my 'grumpy' midwife had gone off duty at ten and had not informed anyone that I was there! — Was this deliberate?

The two midwives could see how distressed I had become and quickly calmed me down and rushed me to the labour ward. They were wonderful and had obviously picked up on the fact that I was terrified of being alone and they never left my side for one minute. They kept telling me that I was a good girl and was doing very well and puffing in time with me. Minutes later I gave birth to a beautiful baby girl! The two mid-wives cheered as they held her up for me to see and told me that I had been very brave.

I decided to have my second child at home, which was a lot better. I was in my own surroundings and at least this time I could be sure that I wouldn't be left on the loo!"

Doreen's Story

WOMEN SHOULD BE PREPARED
WITH SENSIBLE FACTS AND KNOWLEDGE!

Doreen was thirty two when she had her first child, which was considered to be quite old in those days. Here is her account of childbirth . . .

"I am now sixty five years old and I had my first child at the age of thirty two, as I was thirty before I married — very old back then! My mother had always frightened me about the horrors of childbirth, so I was not looking forward to it one little bit — maybe that's why I left it so late!

I had to go to the hospital for three-week bed rest because of high blood pressure before my daughter Paula was born and I believe that the fact that I was terrified about the birth was a contributing factor to this. The Matron of the hospital had a nice idea of bringing around the new-born babies to show the mothers-to-be and to give us some reassurance that it would all be worth it in the end.

One afternoon, while I was resting, I heard the most awful screams echoing down the corridor.

'Oh my Goodness' I thought, if that was what childbirth was like, I couldn't face it! All the other mother's looked horrified as well. We later found out that what we had heard was a young girl aged about seventeen, who had been bought in from a brothel. She was so dirty that it took four nurses to hold her down and wash her clean — hence the screaming! Unfortunately we also found out later than her baby had died shortly after the birth.

I had a very long labour and my husband was kept well away from it all, as husbands were in those days. The actual birth was not too bad as I recall and far less painful than my mother had described anyway!

A few weeks later, I suffered post-natal depression and had to go away to recover, leaving my baby and my husband behind which was very upsetting, but I didn't really have any choice in the matter and I knew that I had to get myself better.

During this time, my baby was christened without me being there. As you can imagine I felt so bad about this. I was then advised not to have anymore children, as it appeared too great a shock to my system.

However, four years later I sailed through a second pregnancy and had no after effects and a lovely little boy. I felt that my family was complete, a boy and a girl, but five years later and at the grand old age of forty one, I found out that I was pregnant again. Unfortunately this time I miscarried — it was just not meant to be.

I cannot say that my brushes with pregnancy have been happy ones, but then I wonder sometimes if there was something deep in my subconscious telling me that it was going to be awful. My children on the other hand are a pleasure and have given me so much joy. That Matron was right; it was all worth it!

My personal opinions of childbirth are that I think women should be provided with sensible facts and knowledge about woman's greatest role in life."

Margaret's Story

TEN DAYS IN O'BLOCK!

Margaret has three sons, all born in the sixties and says that all her experiences were different — the worst being the first born . . .

"I went into hospital on the Saturday night as my labour pains had started and were getting to the point that I felt I could hold out no more! I was pre-booked into a hospital in Bristol, but when we arrived the door was locked. My husband rang the bell and when it was opened, they just let my husband put my suitcase just inside the door and told him to go.

By Monday night, I was still having bad pains and they decided to transfer me to another hospital in the early hours of the Tuesday morning. I was put into a room on my own and a nurse called in every so often. By now I was drugged up and still in a lot of pain as I wanted to keep bearing down, so I found it easier just to sit on the end of the bed.

I can still remember the nurse telling me off every time she came in. 'Lie down Mrs. Smith!', then she would go again. At about 5.30 the following morning, the doctors did their rounds and I heard one say to the other 'Let's go and get some breakfast and then do a forceps on this one!' I had no other information other than this and was terrified as to what was going to happen to me.

Thankfully, the birth was fine, but our baby had to put somewhere away from me for so many hours and I didn't know why, they just said that this was hospital policy with a forceps delivery.

I was then taken to a new maternity ward, which hadn't been opened long and the whole place was lovely, very nice and all fresh. When they bought my baby in to see me later, he was as lovely as I had imagined, but when they checked to see if I was all right, they found that I had a high temperature and an infection.

I was immediately transferred to an isolation unit called O'BLOCK, where I was to spend the next ten days. Ten days in O'BLOCK was agonising, but worth the wait when I was eventually allowed to go home.

With my second child, I also went into hospital because of the problems that I had encountered with the infection, but all was well and I didn't see O'BLOCK again!

When our third son was born, I was told that I couldn't go to the hospital because they needed it for emergencies and as my second birth had gone well, I was to have a home delivery. The only problem with this was that it was the middle of November and we didn't have any central heating, just a coal fire that also heated the water. Thankfully I had a very kind midwife who made me up a single bed in the front room where my son was born.

Nowadays I wouldn't have thought twice to insist that this happened, but one was a little afraid of midwives and doctors and felt that one had to ask their permission!

My poor husband spent that entire birth running back and forth to the telephone box to report on my progress to the doctor and I think he was more exhausted than I was and I was the one giving birth!"

Barbara's Story

"GO TO THE OPERATING THEATRE!"

My own mum, Barbara, has had four children and says that each birth was completely different. The most astounding difference was between my older brother, Richard now thirty four and my younger brother Matthew, now thirteen . . .

"When I discovered that I was expecting my son Richard, our first child, I had been married for just over two years. We lived in a flat — or rather an attic at the top of an old house and I still remember that every time a lorry went by on the road outside, the floor shook uncontrollably!

My husband John was serving in the Royal Air Force at the time and we had just received his posting to Singapore of all places, so I spent most of my pregnancy alone and what a lonely time it was.

I worked in the offices of Eskimo Frozen Foods who had just installed a 'state of the art' computer, the size of a football pitch! We were entering the age of new technology and inventions.

When I finished work, I would go home to a lonely, cold flat but looked forward to the weekends when I could travel back to see my family in Birmingham. It meant an eight hour journey to get there, but I couldn't stand talking to the walls for the whole weekend!

I would be heavily pregnant and walking the streets of Birmingham at two o'clock in the morning, but I felt safe. There wasn't the violence that there is today and you could walk the streets after midnight and not fear for your life.

I do remember being absolutely terrified about telling my mum that I was expecting a baby. I don't know why, I hadn't done anything wrong. John and I had been married for two years, but in those days discussions about sex were still taboo and I remember saying it as quickly as I could, almost as if I was talking about the weather! Mum didn't say very much and I don't think I even told my Dad — I left that up to mum.

My pregnancy was just as a textbook — morning sickness, quickly followed by indigestion and heartburn. I think I kept the indigestion tablet companies in business single-handed. Although, I didn't bloom as most mothers-to-be did — in fact I just felt fat and sick all the time!

The antenatal care wasn't up to much either and I only attended one class, which was run by a sixty-year-old spinster — like she knew what I was going through!

John managed to get home two days before our son arrived and helped massage my back when my labour pains started. I spent the night tossing and turning and got up to go to the loo to find that I had a 'show'.

I woke John up and we made our way to the hospital, which was the equivalent of Faulty Towers! It had an impressive name — Craft Baker Maternity Hospital, but was really a huge old house with no resident doctor and just lots of auxiliary nurses and a Matron in charge.

As the pains progress, I didn't really know what to do with myself and was eventually taken to the delivery room. Thankfully the pain was not too bad and my labour relatively short. John was not allowed in and I don't think I would have wanted him there anyway, although it did feel rather odd having all these strangers around while I was giving birth.

Richard John was born weighing 6lb 7oz and I remember a nurse placing him in my arms. I was filled with such a surge of wonderment that I had never felt before.

Despite my son being born at 3.15pm, I had to wait for four hours to be stitched up as Cleethorpes was shrouded in a blanket of fog and the doctor couldn't get to the hospital! I lay there on this operating table for four hours, feeling all manner of emotions — euphoria at the birth, trembling beyond control from shock and desperately wanting to see my husband, who incidentally had no idea where I was and had been told to stay in the visitors room.

John didn't know what to expect when a nurse abruptly told him to go to the operating theatre! He came in looking as white as a sheet, not knowing quite what to expect as they hadn't bothered to tell him that he had a healthy son and that I was fine! He thought that I must be at deaths door or knocking on heaven's door!

There were lots of rules and regulations and you had to stay in the hospital bed for ten days before you could even go to the toilet by yourself — the most uncomfortable bedpans! The midwifery care could have been better and I can think of at least one nurse who would have been better suited as a jailer!

Visiting was restricted to husbands and immediate family only — husbands two hours and immediate family only for an hour in the afternoon. When I was allowed 'parole' a nurse carried my son to the car and I was pushed in a wheel chair — Craft Baker Maternity Hospital, may I never pass your way again!

I had my second daughter Deborah-Anne in 1968 in Germany as John had been posted there. This was strange because when I went into labour, I had to make my own way to the hospital on a bus whose passengers included six men from all different nationalities — I did think about calling her United Nations!

My second daughter Helen was born back in England and I was more use to how hospitals operated by then and found that I wasn't so bullied as with the first one, but It wasn't until I unexpectedly found out that I was pregnant at the age of forty two that I really saw a change in the way things were done . . ."
(*See 1980 births*)

Julia's Story

'THERE SIMPLY ISN'T ENOUGH INFORMATION FOR WOMEN!'

Julia had all her children in a maternity hospital in Bristol in the years 1966, '67 and '68. She believes that although there wasn't a lot of information available to women back then, there still isn't enough information today . . .

"I don't remember anyone ever suggesting a home-delivery for any of my children. In fact for my first child I don't remember being given a choice. I think it was automatically a ten-day stay for the first baby, regardless of circumstances. For the others I was given the choice to come home after a three day period, but this had to be decided when you booked your bed — very early on in pregnancy.

I remember the antenatal care being very good and in the first few months I was seen by my GP and only had one hospital appointment. As the pregnancy progressed, I attended the hospital more and more frequently and it was a weekly outing by the end of the pregnancy.

During my first pregnancy, I remember being very apprehensive. No one really explained anything to me and I wasn't quite sure of what was suppose to happen. The hospital appointments consisted of being prodded and poked, blood pressure being taken and endless blood samples. Even when I was admitted on bed rest for the last two weeks, I wasn't altogether sure why.

I was induced with my first baby after my two weeks resting period and this was done by intravenous fluids. Still, my labour seemed to last forever and I remember being left on my own for hours and hours on end.

The actual delivery took place with me on my side with a bully of a midwife insisting that I rolled over every time I wanted to push. After the delivery, during which I had an episostomy, I was left alone again for what seemed like ages in a very undignified position of my legs high up in stirrups. When if felt as though my legs would fall off with cramp, someone finally came to stitch me.

I am sure that I felt every bit of it, but to be honest, I was past caring! If I had remembered every detail of that delivery, I'm sure that I wouldn't have had another child — maybe we are equipped to forget it to enable us to carry on the reproduction cycle!

The other thing that I remember was breast-feeding. There was no choice in the matter — unless you were a pretty awful mother, you would breast-feed! I did not find this a particularly pleasant experience and because I had a rather large baby, I didn't have sufficient milk and so had to supplement every feed with a bottle. When I came home, I gave up the breast-feeding and my son went straight on to the bottle!

When I had my other children, fashions had changed and no pressure was put upon me to breast-feed, in fact I would say that it veered more towards to the bottle. My son was fed on Carnation tinned milk and thrived on it!

My third child was still born and not something that I want to dwell on, but when I had my last child in 1968, life on the maternity wards had become more and more relaxed and the essence was more on what the mother wanted. Some mothers were even having their husbands at the birth! This was not actively encouraged though and I remember my husband having to sign a form prior to the birth to say that if he attended and fainted, the hospital would not be held responsible for him as it was not their job!

I didn't actually want my husband there and he didn't want to attend. Rather like periods and sanitary protection, in those days all that was 'women's stuff' and I can't blame the men for not wanting to be a part of it!

Barbara's Story

"I BEGGED THE NURSE TO LET ME DIE!"

Barbara now sixty seven had her first child Mark in 1962 and was in so much agony that she said she just wanted to die . . .

"I was thirty two years old when I had my first child Mark and considered then to be an older mum-to-be! My labour lasted twenty four hours and I was originally due to have him at home, which I was told was usual back then.

The midwife who was looking after me got very worried when I started to bleed and I believe that this was down to her trying to break my waters unsuccessfully — she was very young and inexperienced.

I was taken to the hospital and by this time I was out of my mind with the pain and with nothing to relieve it, I begged the nurse to just let me die there and then. The doctor listened to the baby's heartbeat and I knew that something was wrong because I heard him say, so many cc's of Pethidine and forceps.

The midwife at the hospital then said 'I'm going to cut you now, you won't need an anaesthetic.' Then she took a giant pair of scissors to me and the doctor literally dragged my baby out by his head!

I had no more energy, yet all the time I could hear someone screaming. I then realised that it was actually me screaming! They did show me my son who was very pale but beautiful — he was probably half scared to death at his mother screaming her head off!

When the nurses bought the babies round to be fed, mine wasn't there and I asked if he was alright. They said that he couldn't be disturbed for a few hours, as he's had a bad time during the birth. When my husband came to the hospital, I asked him if he had seen our son and he said that he was covered up in a crib.

I knew nothing of this and I naturally thought that something was wrong with him. I had seen him for a split second and then he was taken away with no explanation.

When I was allowed to take him home, I was stitched inside and out, yet had no help from anyone. I didn't know when I should feed him and didn't feed him until the day after we arrived home — no wonder he cried so much! You tend to think that a mother knows instinctively what to do with her baby, but I didn't!

My second childbirth experience fourteen months later was just as uncaring. The two nurses that attended me were busy chatting about a dance that they had been to the night before, while I was begging for some help to ease the pain. They stopped their conversation for one of them to say 'Look! There's gas and air beside you!' I felt so un-cared for. Maternity hospitals were just conveyer belts for pregnant women.

With my third child, I was adamant that it was going to be born at home and I had a wonderful midwife who advised me through every stage of my labour.

In those days you didn't argue with the doctors or nurses. It was seen as a very exclusive profession. Knowing what I do today, I would have cause to sue the medical profession for the lack of care that I received, but you didn't question it back then!"

CHAPTER FOUR
1970's

One of the most important times in a woman's life is when she has a child, yet the care and understanding from many hospitals was still seen to be very poor in the seventies.

Mother's reported that they were not being told what had happened to their babies after they had given birth and many women suffered mentally and physically at the hands of the medical staff.

Read Jenny's heart-breaking story of her experience and the reason why Irene defiantly locked herself in the loo . . .

Jenny's Story

"I NEVER GOT TO HOLD MY PRECIOUS BABY"

Jenny, now forty six debated whether or not to write her story, but decided that she would if only to let people know that the care that she received was in fact careless . . .

"I am now forty seven, and I married my husband in 1972. After four years, we were expecting our first baby. The year was 1976. From very early on I felt that that there was something amiss with my pregnancy. Whether you would call it women's intuition, I do not know, all I do know is that I felt very uneasy about the whole thing.

The weeks passed and on various occasions I voiced my thoughts, only to be told, more or less, that I did not know what I was talking about, as I had not been pregnant before.

The end of June came and I visited the antenatal clinic. On the last few visits, the doctors had to try really hard to find the heart-beat, using one of those ear-trumpet things. I mentioned that all the movements, of which there had not been too many, were in reverse i.e. the kicking sensations were in my lower stomach.

'Nonsense' came the reply; 'The baby has just turned that's all'. So I went home.

That was the Monday afternoon and in the early hours of July 1st, I started to have pains. We drove to the hospital, which was a small cottage hospital, just outside of Staffordshire and we arrived at about 4.30 in the morning

As soon as the Sister examined me, I could tell that she was concerned. She left me then came back and said that a doctor would be with me soon. Apparently, she thought that the baby was in the breech position. I continued to have really painful contractions and now my husband was not allowed in and had to stand outside in the corridor.

When the doctor arrived, he turned out to be our own doctor, who was on call that night. He advised me that they were going to transfer me to a hospital in Burton. I asked him how far away it was and he replied forty miles! I then said that I didn't think that I would make it in time, but all the same off they went, leaving me alone again.

My husband was oblivious to all of this and didn't know what was going on. The doctor returned to examine me and he could see that my concern was genuine. There really was no time to transfer me.

Eventually, after the, may I say more than usual grunts and groans and without any gas and air, my baby was born at 5.57am.

I was stitched up with quite a few stitches and my baby was placed into a cot at the other side of the room. I didn't even get the chance to hold him.

While the Sister was cleaning me up, my son made attempts to cry and I remarked that I thought he needed picking up. The Sister left the room and returned to say that they were going to take the baby, who seemed to be having breathing difficulties, to another hospital in Sutton Coldfield. By now it was about seven in the morning and I briefly saw my husband, who consequently went to the hospital with our baby.

After a short time, I was moved into a ward with other mothers who all had their babies with them. You cannot imagine how I felt. No one said anything and at around ten that morning, I asked if I could use the phone to try and find out where my husband was.

I rang my sister who lived some twenty miles away, thinking that my husband had gone to spread the news that we had a son. That was upsetting, having to tell my sister that I did not know what was going on.

Just before 11.30 that same morning, a nurse came and told me that they would be taking me down to my own room — still saying nothing about my baby.

At around midday my husband came back and I immediately knew that something was wrong.

My baby had died.

He told me that the doctors had fought to save his life and we had heard all sorts of stories and reasons as to why this awful thing had happened to us, eventually making us feel like we had given birth to a freak.

My husband said that he would return home and get me some things, but then at around four that afternoon, I was taken home in an ambulance. It was as though they didn't know what else to do with me, they had done their job.

My husband got the shock of his life when I walked in and so we were left to our own devices, not knowing what to do or think.

After a couple of weeks, we were sent an appointment to see a paediatrician who told us that our baby had been born without any kidneys. He said that it was very unusual for this to happen and when we told him about all the reasons the doctors and nurses had given us at the time, he was quite horrified. We were also told that had our own doctor not been there that night, who was also a qualified surgeon, I might not have lived either.

I never got to hold my precious baby. I never even got to have a good look at him and to this day, we still do not know what happened to his body.

Over the years we have thought that we should try to find out, but we have also been told that sometimes they do not even bury tiny new-born babies. We feel that we could not cope with anything other than a burial place.

The feelings of guilt that we did not do enough to find out what went wrong are very strong, but on the other hand, we lost our baby and nothing would ever change that.

All the happenings over that weekend were in a sort of haze and we were carried along with a mist, just drifting along, not knowing what to say to each other. It was as though it had not been real — but it had."

NOTE: *When Jenny wrote to me, she ended saying that she did not know if the events that happened to her and her husband would be of use, but that it is a part of their lives that will never be forgotten.*

Irene's Story

"I DEFIANTLY LOCKED MYSELF IN THE LOO UNTIL THEY LISTENED TO ME!'

Irene explains why she had to lock herself in the loo to be heard ...

"Nothing would ever persuade me to repeat the experience of my birth with my daughter. Despite her now being twenty five years old, I can still remember every detail as if it were only yesterday!

So what was so awful, that it prevented me from ever having another baby? Well, in hindsight, I admit that it was partly my own fault because I had insisted on being booked into a small cottage hospital, which held no doctors, only midwives. I felt at the time that it would be cosier than a large general hospital.

The day that I was admitted (Friday), I had been having pains since the early morning, so at lunchtime, my husband took me to the hospital, by which time the pains were regular and strong. When I was shown onto the ward, I got my first clue that I had made a terrible mistake in my choice of hospital. There were no curtains at the windows!

Later that day, my suspicions were confirmed when the midwife, who made no attempt to screen the bed off, gave me an internal examination. The bare windows left me in full view of visitors who walked past my ward to other areas of the hospital. A rather humiliating experience to say the least!

Following the usual practice in those days, I was shaved and given an enema. This led to my second humiliating experience. The enema did not have the desired effect and left me coiled up in agony. I was then placed into a bath of hot water and what should have taken place in the toilet, happened in the bath, which I found particularly distressing.

That evening, my husband came to visit me and as the ward was very close, we could hear another woman screaming with pain and it left me feeling terrified.

All during the following day, I was still having regular pains, but nothing developed. I was examined several times and one occasion still stands out in my mind. The midwife was so rough and literally shoved her fingers inside me so strongly that I flinched and yelped with pain.

Eventually I was transferred to a side ward and kept under sedation. Whenever I woke up and complained about the pain, I was given another injection to send me back to sleep. Other than that I was left very much alone.

By Sunday, I was feeling very isolated. In the afternoon, just before visiting time I left the room to use the toilet. Passing the front door, I saw my sister walk in. I was so relieved to see a friendly face that I cried. At that moment a nurse arrived and told my sister to wait outside, as it wasn't visiting time for another two minutes!

During the early hours of Monday morning, I begged the staff to ring my GP at home, as I knew that he would have to pass the hospital in order to reach the surgery. All during my hospital stay, I was made to feel as if I was a complete nuisance because my delivery wasn't going according to the book — My baby must have been reading the wrong book!

Looking back I wonder why I put up with the treatment that I got, I can only remember that I was feeling very vulnerable and at the mercy of the hospital staff that I did not want to make a fuss.

The final insult came after the visit from my GP, who incidentally did not mind coming to see me at all and said that had he been called he would have come on the Sunday. He advised me to transfer to the general hospital and I clearly heard him say that a nurse should travel with me. When the ambulance arrived, the Sister said that I was to go alone. By this stage I didn't care, I was just glad to get away.

Unfortunately, my arrival hardly filled me with renewed confidence as I was left on a trolley in a corridor for quite some time. Things did begin to improve when a nice doctor and nurse treated me with such tender care and this restored my faith in the medical profession. The nurse even stayed after her shift because she could see how frightened I had become.

My daughter was eventually born by caesarean section that

evening at nine o'clock.

Although my treatment immediately before and after the birth couldn't be faulted, things soon went down hill. My daughter was placed in intensive care and I was on my own in a side ward, where I was put into the care of an elderly nurse, who also had a bad back!

Because of the extensive stitching across my stomach, I could hardly move and the nurse was supposed to help me out of bed. Because of her back problem, she couldn't support me and so left me perched on the side of a chair. The pain was incredible and tears were streaming down my face. Thankfully a doctor passed by and ordered her to get me back into bed immediately.

During this time, I was bought food, but it was left at the other end of the room where I couldn't reach it and I spent the day not being able to get anything to eat. Eventually the nice nurse who attended the birth helped me by feeding me cold rice pudding. I didn't actually like cold rice pudding, but on that occasion it tasted delicious!

My daughter was released from intensive care where she had been fed on warm milk. Now that she was on the ward, she was expected to conform to a strict regime of being fed at four hourly intervals, with cold milk straight from the fridge. As a result, she was never ready to feed and began to lose weight.

I was in hospital for three weeks, during which time my daughter continued to lose weight. I begged the staff to give her warm milk, but they refused saying that it was too time consuming.

Feeling more assertive and ready for a fight, I defiantly locked myself in the toilet and refused to come out until they listened to me. They did!

I discharged myself immediately, leaving my baby in their care and immediately told my GP the whole story. He investigated the story and my daughter was given warm milk and fed on demand.

Four years later my sister had her own baby in the same hospital, but sadly nothing had changed.

To this day my daughter still does not like cold drinks and as a child insisted on drinking hot orange juice. The whole incident put me off ever having another child. The lack of care and understanding was terrible — I just hope things have improved over the last twenty five years!

CHAPTER FIVE
1980's

Thankfully, things were improving for mothers-to-be and not before time! With the help from the National Childbirth Trust, women were better informed of what they could expect and what pain relief was available to them if they required it.

Women were encouraged to give birth to their babies in the way that they felt most comfortable and were helped when feeding their new-borns. For the first time encouragement was also given for father's to attend antenatal classes and the birth of their child. Maternity staff were educated properly so that the mothers and babies needs were met and child-care education was readily available.

Read Lesley's story, who describes her childbirth as a 'wonderful experience' and how Joanne found the 'missing ingredient' to help her have the baby she longed for . . .

Lesley's Story

"ALL IN ALL, A WONDERFUL EXPERIENCE!"

Lesley, now forty nine, gave birth on October 13th 1984 at the age of thirty four to her first and only child. She says that her childbirth experience was far from being a horror story . . .

"From the age of between 18 and 22, I had been on the birth pill. During a previous marriage I had conceived at the age of 26, but I miscarried early at just eight weeks.

I had been feeling broody and the urge to procreate and have a baby dominated my life from about the age of 25 to 28. My husband co-operated in fertility tests and it turned out that his sperm count was low. I was tested and it proved that there was nothing wrong with my reproductive organs. We declined AIH and AID, but eventually the marriage broke down, mainly due to the stresses of infertility and eventually we went our separate ways.

In 1983, I had left my husband, my home and my job and moved back to Scotland. Subsequently, I met the man who is now my husband and the father of our child.

I conceived on January 26th 1984. How can I be so sure? We were snow-bound that day (records confirm the weather conditions in Scotland) and we spent the day in bed! When I missed my period and got a positive result on a home-pregnancy test, I took advantage of the leap year and proposed to the father-to-be. He was even more surprised than I was! After almost ten years of infertility, I had given up any hope of ever becoming a mother.

At the age of thirty four and with one miscarriage behind me, I was nervous about my pregnancy. I did not dare hope that it would reach fruition. Especially when I threatened a miscarriage before twelve weeks. However, apart from that one scare, the pregnancy progressed without so much as a single morning's sickness. As I got bigger, I would get chronic cramps in my legs upon awakening, but I can honestly say that was the worst thing about it.

I was living in Edinburgh and attending all the pre-natal classes. My employers were very helpful and allowed me time off work, but it wasn't easy. I was an un-married mother-to-be when I made a business trip to Stornoway, on the Isle of Lewis and heavily pregnant, so I was always careful to wear a wedding band in order to consider the sensibilities of others. (You can't even hang your washing out on a Sunday up there, never mind run around advertising the fact that you're about to have a child out of wedlock!)

Throughout my pregnancy, I blossomed. I felt and looked wonderful. During August I had to make a business trip to England. It was a very hot, humid summer and I wilted like a limp lettuce leaf. But baby and I bonded and I got quite attached to my 'bump'. I spoke to him, touched him and sang to him — I was looking forward to meeting my baby.

Our baby was due to be delivered in Edinburgh, but four weeks before the birth, we moved south and I found myself in Leamington Spa. In fact, we did not get the keys to our flat until the day before I went into hospital. While I was in hospital, my husband and his friends moved everything in. Talk about bad planning!

I went into labour in the early hours of Saturday, 13th October. I rose from our bed and went through to a quiet room. The only light was from a digital clock, which I watched to time my contractions, which were coming very quickly, right from the start.

The contractions were actually painless, just strong muscular movements and I just rocked on my hands and knees and let the sensations flow. I had read an interesting passage in a book about childbirth which explained that the sensation of pain is only felt when friction is caused by resisting the muscular movement. So I was determined not to resist it and it was painless.

When the contractions became stronger, I woke my husband and my waters broke before the ambulance arrived. When the ambulance came, I waddled out in my dressing gown and slippers. They lay me down, took one look at me and instructed me to pant! I was so dilated, they felt that the baby would arrive before they got me to the hospital.

Happily the baby was lying in the prime position for giving birth, so everything was going according to plan. They wheeled me down into the delivery room and didn't even bother with shaving me. The midwives joked that they were due to leave their shift at eight that morning and could I possibly accommodate them!

Having previously eaten a Chinese meal, I was burping and feeling sick. I became so fed up that I told them to do something and quick before I threw up all over the place. I was given a peppermint cordial to drink which did help. One midwife kept telling me to push. I told her that I would push when I felt good and ready and not a moment before! I don't think she was use to being spoken to like that — One of the advantages of being thirty-something — not easily intimidated!

Just before the baby was due to arrive, a doctor told me to stop pushing because it looked like I might tear and I was more than happy to let him administer a J-Cut.

Well John, as we named him, shot out like a jet-propelled rocket! (He's been in a hurry ever since!)

The whole process took just three hours from start to finish and all this from a thirty four year old woman. Not so much as a whiff of Oxygen and the midwives were able to leave their shift on time!

John was 5lb 2oz, light for his dates and needed to be kept in hospital for a week while we established feeding and he put on weight. The staff were brilliant, so too was the lady from the NCT who helped me with breast-feeding. All in all a wonderful experience."

Joanne's Story

'ZINC HELPED ME HAVE THE BABY I SO LONGED FOR'

Joanne had lost three babies to miscarriage and had given up all hope of having another baby. Here is her story . . .

"I miscarried three times, all very painful experiences, both physical and emotional. I just didn't seem to be able to hold on to my babies — although I'm sure one seemed to be triggered off by an ultra sound scan, which seemed quite painful at the time (pressing too hard).

The baby I lost was five and a half months, a little boy and he seemed quite comfy up until that scan. When I lost him, the hospital in Cornwall was lovely and the nurses very caring. They cleaned him up and wrapped him up in a shawl. They made sure that I knew that he would never recover and then they gave him me to cuddle for as long as I wanted. This was so important to me. I could say goodbye to him and tell him how sorry I was.

I gave up all hope of ever having another child. I was getting too old for bringing up a baby. Then at the age of thirty nine, I became pregnant again! In the meantime I had read an article in a magazine, which said that there was some connection between the lack of Zinc and miscarriages.

I had always had a Zinc deficiency and even as a child I had white blobs in my nails. So I took extra Zinc to see if it would help and it did.

My daughter is now eight years old. She has always done everything at great speed, including childbirth — she took just 1 hour and 23 minutes to be delivered, from me waking up in the night with labour pains. We only just made it to the hospital and the nurses were wonderful in helping me to look after my beloved little girl.

I just couldn't put my baby down. Nothing else in the world mattered. I breast-fed her for a long time, because I also read that this can help to give the right nutrients to help the brain and give a good platform for intelligence. I believe that this is true, as she is a very intelligent little girl, already having jumped a class at school.

I often wonder if she would ever be here today if I hadn't taken the Zinc tablets. I am sure that other women in physical ways similar to myself will benefit from this advice, if they too are prone to miscarriage. I am sure it helped me and I have my little girl to prove it!"

Barbara's Story

"TWENTY YEARS AND ONE DAY BETWEEN MY FIRST AND LAST CHILD!"

My own mother Barbara thought that after having three children and in her forties, her child bearing days were over — boy, did she have a shock . . .

"When I found out that I was expecting another baby at the age of 42, I already had my first son, Richard who was 20 and in the army, my daughter Deborah who was 18 and at college and my youngest daughter Helen, who was still at school studying for her exams.

I thought at first that it must be the menopause, because my periods had stopped and never contemplated that I could be expecting, so when my GP confirmed that I was in fact five months pregnant, I just didn't know what to think. I had been advised earlier to change my contraceptive pill to the mini-pill, which I'm sure contributed to me getting pregnant again! — The doctor even said that he would arrange an abortion right away, because he felt the same.

My first thoughts were how my, grown up family were going to take the news! My husband John said that he would support me with whatever I decided to do. My eldest daughter was over the moon and wanted to know when the baby was due. My son was quite keen that it would be a boy so that they could play football together! — I think he always felt left out because he had two sisters! My youngest daughter was absolutely disgusted by the idea and I remember her saying 'Mother, how could you do this to me, when I've got exams to get through too!' I'm sure we swapped roles with each other. It should have been me telling her to go careful! I don't think she could understand that her father and I still had a romantic relationship!

Once the dust had settled and the news had spread throughout the small village — this was the hardest bit to cope with, all the villagers voicing their disapproval, although not directly to me. I decided that it was meant to be and actually quite liked the idea of having another baby to care for. Both my husband and I had come from big families and I liked the idea of having four children. After all, my three were almost independent now.

I did worry about anything happening to me or John and the long age gap between the children, but I guess I just thought that it was meant to be and as long as I could give it all my love, everything would be just fine.

The summer of 1985 was a particularly hot one and I carried my son throughout the hot summer. I couldn't get comfortable and avoided the sun as much as possible, but other than that my pregnancy went well, despite all the warnings about my age. I think that by the time I had found out that I was expecting, I was already five months pregnant and so only had a few months to prepare, and consequently not much time to dwell on it.

My baby's birth date was for the 10th of October and on the night of 6th; feeling fat and fed up, my daughter went out and bought me a Chinese meal to cheer me up. It was my older son's twentieth birthday that day and I was worn out from shopping for birthday presents, so I was glad to just put my feet up for the evening.

Sometime during the night, I awoke and desperately needed the loo, only to find that I'd had a show and that labour pains had set in. That was it, I knew that the baby was coming, and I woke John up and told him to call for the ambulance immediately. Deborah woke up as I was standing on the stairs and wanted to come with me, but I told her to stay and look after the house and her sister and I would call her from the hospital.

The ambulance arrived and I was now worried that the baby was going to come before we made it to the hospital. We got just inside the delivery room, when my son was born and the only problem we incurred was that his cord got twisted around his neck, but the medical staff managed to free him straight away.

Twenty years and one day after my first son was born, I had a second son, who we named Matthew John. He weighed just over 5lbs and I didn't need any stitches — not bad for a women in her forties!

I found the changes remarkable between my two son's births. The care in the hospital was wonderful and a lovely doctor told me to stay for as long as I wanted, but after a week I wanted to get home to my family.

Another big difference was the attitude to visiting. When I had my eldest son, it was restricted to fathers only. This time everyone was welcomed and my daughters regularly visited out of hours.

My son Matthew is now nearly fourteen and a real joy to have around. He has his older brother and his sisters close by who spoil him rotten and I have never for one moment regretted having him so late in life. In fact I feel that I can devote more time and attention to him because I am more mature and can appreciate every day that I have with him. I am sure that this was something that was meant to be.

Caroline's Story

"SINGLE MOTHER Vs MARRIED MOTHER"

Caroline, now thirty one, found the most resounding difference between her two children's births was the time factor and the attitudes of the staff from being a single mother in 1984 to a married mother in 1993 . . .

"When I was expecting my first child Alex, I wasn't married and all the women were called Mrs. and I clearly remember, when they called my surname, I use to look around for my mum!

I think I was treated differently to the married women in the clinic and at the hospital, despite it being the eighties. I was unmarried and only seventeen at the time and this was recorded on my records. Although attitudes towards to illegitimate children were far more relaxed than years ago, there was still, and I believe still is, a stigma attached to being a single mother. You're classed as if you're a classic case for the social services and you've had a bad up bringing.

When I was in labour with my son, I asked the hospital to phone my mum, but they kept telling me that it would be ages before he arrived. They eventually did call her, but by the time my parents had arrived it was all over. Alex was only 4lbs 10oz and losing body temperature and was whisked away from me just after the birth.

The following day a consultant came to visit me and discuss contraception. I told him that this was the last thing on my mind as I no longer had a partner and if and when I did want to use any, I would contact my GP. He then said with a laugh that he would see me in nine months time! As you can imagine, I was devastated by this attitude. It was as if it was expected of me to just keep getting pregnant, all because of a simple accident. I think this contributed to my post-natal depression that I suffered after the birth.

My experience with my daughter Chloe's birth nine years

later, was completely different and a very happy experience, although I was still a little apprehensive at first. By this time I had got married and antenatal classes were more informal, with everyone being called by their first name only. Just knowing that my records showed that I was now a Mrs. made a huge difference to me and gave me that extra bit of confidence.

I also had the same midwife throughout my care, which was nice because I could relate to her and she knew all about me.

I kept a detailed birth plan of just what I wanted at the birth and Chris, my husband stayed with me the whole time. I had an Epidural and couldn't feel my contractions, so I asked if I could have a mirror so that I could watch the birth and could see when I had to push. Chloe was born a healthy 7lbs 10oz and I was much more relaxed and had no post-natal depression this time.

I think that with your second child, you tend to feel more confident and you do ask yourself why you let people treat you so awfully the first time around. You are determined to demand what you want the second time around and the attitude of the staff is more of what you, the mother wants, rather than telling you what you want!"

CHAPTER SIX
1990's

This decade, we are at our best in medical technology with regards to childbirth and despite some women still experiencing the odd problem with maternity staff, the majority have been happy with the births of their children.

Caesarean Sections are now considered to be one of the safest methods of childbirth, for both mother and child should problems occur during childbirth and more women are actually asking for Elective Caesareans.

Many women are speaking up for themselves and demanding the birth that they want, and getting it. Home births are once again popular, but this time by choice rather than to save on resources. More and more information is widely available to women via magazines especially designed for the pregnant woman and new mother and the social care is the best that you could ask for.

Read my own account of childbirth, when after being advised that I should have my first daughter by caesarean, I decided to have the second one the same way. Ruth was determined to have a home-birth with her son Oliver and Wendy experienced her childbirth in two different countries . . .

Wendy's Story

"GERMANY V ENGLAND"

Women's experiences of childbirth not only differ from period of time, but also from country to country. Wendy, 38 and a scientist, had one child in Germany and an unexpected home-birth with her second child in England . . .

"My first child was born in Germany in 1992, due to me and my husband working and living in Hamburg at the time. Throughout my pregnancy I was cared for by an obstetrician/gynaecologist and although the spacing of appointments was similar to that in the UK the treatment was markedly different.

An internal examination at every visit, three scans and the baby's heat beat monitored at weekly intervals for the last month. There was no real chance of building up any kind of rapport with the medical staff and the community midwife has no role to play in the pregnancy care or even the birth.

Shortly before the birth you are sent a list of midwives and it is up to the future parents to find a midwife who will visit you after you return home from hospital. This is all conducted over the phone and the midwife we chose thought it rather odd that we should want to see her before our child had been born, especially since the health care system would not pay for this visit.

I felt reasonably prepared for the birth and we attended classes at the hospital, which covered the procedures that would take place on arrival. My mother always had a positive view on childbirth, so I think I must have stored this in my subconscious and it gave me the confidence that I needed.

There are no birth plans in Germany; it is left entirely to the couple to decide as they go along what they need. Gas and Air is not used at all and Pethidine it not recommended but is available if required. The main pain relief is an Epidural; so most mothers are encouraged to give birth naturally. We also had to attend a twelve hour course on parenting and taking care of a baby, which is also a requirement in Germany.

I felt very excited about the birth, if somewhat sad that my family were so far away and I was woken in the morning with labour pains on my due date and decided to ignore them. A couple of hours later, I had a rather extended bout of diarrhoea and decided that I should go to the hospital.

When we arrived I was examined and it was decided that I should be taken straight to the delivery room and immediately had a catheter placed into my arm. The room was in a cheery yellow and the medical equipment carefully hidden to make the room as normal looking as possible. All the staff were very friendly and helpful and everything went well apart from when the heat monitor kept falling off my stomach whenever I had a strong contraction. In the end they attached a scalp monitor to the babies head, which was a little worrying at the time.

During this time, my husband was told to keep me supplied with oxygen — apparently this keeps them occupied and stops them fainting! Babies in Germany are always delivered by an obstetrician, not the nursing staff and after a quick delivery the baby and my husband left the room while I was stitched up.

The amusing thing about this was when the doctor came to stitch me up, he bent his head to the task and said 'So you work for Professor so and so then', I thought that I must have it stamped on my thigh or something, but in fact he had remembered my face from a lecture that we had both attended!

Despite it being quite a lonely time in Germany, it was also a nice experience and very typical to those who gave birth in the hospitals in Hamburg.

My daughter's birth, two years later was completely different, not only because we were back in England, but also because she had taken us by surprise which resulted in a home-birth!

I had everything arranged for my son; child-care, food and even equipped myself with a pager, just in case this one was also going to be a quick delivery. I had spent the morning taking my son to the shops and then to the gym club and at about 12.30, I felt a sudden contraction.

I paged everyone who needed to know because they were

suddenly coming very quickly. Fortunately my midwife arrived just as I got home and said that I didn't have time to get to the hospital and so prepared for a home delivery. My bed was covered in absorbent mats and my husband even bought in my son's splat mat!

Twenty minutes later, our daughter arrived! My son slept right through it all and our baby was dressed while I had a warm bath.

I think that I have been really lucky with my experiences. Two relatively painless deliveries and two very different styles of birth and I would certainly opt for a home delivery again. I shall certainly endeavour to give my own daughter the same positive advice that my mother gave me. Oh and by the way, I did throw out the splat mat!

Deborah's Story

'TWO CAESAREAN BIRTHS —
TWO BEAUTIFUL DAUGHTERS'

My own children were both born by elective caesarean section and were truly wonderful experiences . . .

"My own account of childbirth is one of a great deal of pleasure and thankfully very little pain. My daughters are both nineties babies, the first being born on 9th December 1993 and the second three years later on 3rd September 1996, a time when medical technology had overwhelmed us.

I remember, having heard all the horror stories about childbirth I was terrified at the prospect of having a baby — I am not good with pain, even a cut finger sends me dizzy, so how on earth was I going to manage having a baby! So I was secretly pleased when my consultant last examined me and recommended that I have a caesarean delivery because my daughter was lying in the breech position and would not turn at such a late stage. Added to this the fact that I am only five foot tall and seven and a half stone contributed to his decision.

My pregnancy was fine, although I found that every time I attended the clinic I was seen by yet another midwife who I had never seen before, but I think this was practice for the area where we lived. I suffered a bit towards the end of the pregnancy with sciatica — a constant, painful ache along the sciatic nerve, but other than that I enjoyed being pregnant.

It was quite amusing when I made an appointment to see my consultant to discuss details of the birth. He looked in his diary, made a mental note that he had golf at the weekend and asked me if the 9th December would be all right. I looked in my diary, made a note that I had the hairdresser's for the following morning and told him that I didn't have anything planned for that day. So the 9th it was to be.

Being a natural born organiser, I was pleased that I had two weeks to get everything sorted out before I went into hospital. I didn't actually know anyone who'd had a caesarean section at the time and all the information I could find out was either in books or pregnancy magazines, which all seemed to portray it in a bad light because it wasn't a natural birth.

In the end I decided that my consultant knew best and reassured myself that he wouldn't have suggested it if it wasn't the best option for me and my baby. I knew that if I dwelled on it too much, I would spend the whole fortnight worrying about it.

I was admitted to the Ashcombe Maternity hospital in Weston-Super-Mare the day before the operation and my husband, little brother and my parents all came in loaded with enough reading material for me to fill a library. The reason that I had to go in the night before was so that my blood could be matched, should I need a blood transfusion.

I cried a lot that night, partly because it was the first night that my husband and I had not spent the night together since the day we met and partly because I missed my puppy Leah — she had been my 'baby' up until that day.

I was given something to make me go to sleep and was woken the following morning by my husband and my mum. I had a brief chat with my appointed midwife, Nicky, who told me that she would be with me throughout the entire operation and she asked my husband if he would like to be present at the birth, to which he bravely agreed — although I'm sure he would have rather been doing something else!

I was prepared for theatre, which meant that I had to be shaved, jewellery taken off, gowned up and my nail polish removed — apparently the medical team can tell how your condition is by the changing in your nails.

I elected to remain awake during the operation because I have always had an aversion to being put to sleep and combined with the fact that I may never wake up again terrified me! So the next stage was for me to have a spinal injection (Epidural) which numbed everything from my chest down and waving a tearful goodbye to my mum who looked as white as a sheet with worry that her 'baby' was going to be slaughtered, I set off towards the sign which read theatre.

I was asked to sit on the edge of the trolley to have the spinal block inserted, which didn't hurt and as I looked up I saw my consultants agenda for the day pinned up on the notice board in front of me. It read . . .

Deborah Durbin . . . Caesarean Section 9am
Julliette Thomas . . . Wisdom Tooth extraction 10am

And I thought this was going to take all day!

The feeling in my legs and tummy soon went and I was prodded and pricked to make sure that I couldn't feel anything and was then taken through to the operating theatre where my husband was waiting with bated breath.

The theatre was busy with the medical team and students preparing for my child's birth. Apparently, my consultant was the best in the business and had a big following whenever he performed a caesarean!

After having a number of sticky patches attached to my arms, legs and chest, a screen was erected across my tummy so that I wouldn't be able to see the operation take place and my husband sat on a stool midway so that he was able to see both my head and the operation.

As I lay there, I felt nothing and was having wonderful a chat with a German midwife who was talking to me the whole time — I'm sure this was to keep my mind off what was going on downstairs!

As we chatted about what we would be doing for Christmas, our conversation was interrupted by the sound of a small cry — our baby girl had been born and I hadn't even noticed!

The staff all applauded and someone grabbed the camera from my husband and took several pictures of our newly born daughter and us together. We were a bit stunned as we were both convinced that I was having a boy and had already decided to call him Liam! So it was a quick decision as to what we were going to call our daughter and both agreed on Rebecca-Marie.

The operation lasted for ten minutes from start to finish — boy what a great birth! It was more like a party in there with all the shouts of congratulations, hug and kisses!

By 11 o'clock, I was back in my room, having spent an hour

in recovery and I found it quite amusing that Mrs. Thomas — Tooth Extraction, was being wheeled in still unconscious from having her tooth taken out as I was recovering from having my daughter.

I was put back into my bed and because I couldn't feel my legs I suddenly noticed that I was lying in bed with both legs wide apart, so I asked my husband if he could please close them!

I was connected to a drip for the night and had two drains attached to drain of any excess fluid that may build up during the night, but the most amazing thing that I discovered was that I noticed that my wound was actually stapled together with what I can only describe as industrial sized metal staples. This was somewhat worrying, but my midwife assured me that I wouldn't ooze out and that they were quite safe.

I am not a tea drinker by nature, but something inside me craved for a cup of tea — well four cups actually but because of body shock I could hardly hold the cup and my mum had to feed me sips of tea. I found out later that body shock is the body's natural reaction to any cut that is deeper than an inch and always responds in the body shaking.

We all slept a lot that day and I felt a bit groggy by the evening as the drugs began to wear off, but the following day I was encouraged to get up and about, by first having help to go to the loo — it was that or use a bed pan and I wasn't about to do that!

I couldn't believe that out of all the women in the hospital, there were only two of us who'd had caesareans and the only two women who kept their babies with them the whole time. The other mothers who'd had their babies naturally refused to look after their babies during the night and put them into the nursery for the whole time that they were there. I kept my daughter with me 24 hours a day, feeding, changing and cuddling her.

I have never been one to wander around for hours in my dressing gown and so would get myself dressed and occasionally pop down to the hospital shop when my husband was cuddling his new daughter. One day I was stopped by one of the midwives and asked who I was coming to visit! She thought that I was actually a visitor rather than a woman who had just had a caesarean section days before! I've always said it's mind over matter!!

I stayed in hospital for five days in total and felt fine when I got back home — although I was advised not to do too much bending down and I wasn't allowed to drive for six weeks which I didn't like.

When I had our second daughter Georgina three years later the hospital where I had Rebecca no longer catered for caesareans, so I had to go to St. Michael's Hospital in Bristol. This time round, I was asked if I would like to try a natural delivery, to which I declined.

My first operation had gone so well that I didn't want to have to endure a painful labour and then an emergency caesarean if things didn't go according to plan, so I said that I would rather have another caesarean birth.

The procedure was much the same, although we did have to wait five hours to be called into theatre due to an emergency.

This time around, I asked my husband to look after Rebecca whilst I went into theatre, which was a little daunting, but the staff there were wonderful and very relaxed about the whole thing. The anaesthetist read his newspaper while the anaesthetic was working its way through and they put the Hits of the 90's tape on to play.

Our second daughter was born to the sounds of 'Take That'.

And so Georgina-Louise was born and we were wheeled out into a rest room   actually it was a converted stock room due to lack of space in the hospital and whilst Georgina was put under a small heater to keep her temperature up I lay there supping tea again!

The only problem that I encountered this time around was that instead of being placed in a single room, I ended up in a ward with three other women due to the lack of space — two of which were under social service care and not very desirable.

I desperately wanted to go home to my husband and other daughter as soon as possible and although Georgina was well enough to go home, I was told that I would have to stay because I had a lot of visible bruising from the delivery. In the end I asked to see a doctor because I felt fine and I really wanted to go home. The doctor confirmed that I was fit to leave, so I did straight away!

Even after just three years the procedure for stitching up was different. With Georgina I had what use to be described as butterfly stitches placed across my stomach. This consisted of a long strip of paper with thousands of dissolvable stitches along it and after three days I was able to peel the paper off in the shower.

All in all I enjoyed both births and despite the bad publicity caesareans have got, I put pay to many of the myths that I had heard. I bonded with my daughters straight away and was back to normal within three weeks of having them both.

As with any method of childbirth you can have a good or a bad experience which will influence your opinions about that particular birth altogether. Thankfully I had two wonderful births.

I am all for medical technology and I am thankful that I had my children the way I did and didn't have to encounter some of the horrific birth stories that I have come across when researching this book!

One thing that I did find interesting about the maternity wards in the nineties is the monitoring of visitors. Since the scare of babies being taken from hospitals, security measures have been fully enforced with cameras and automatically locking doors to all the maternity wards in the UK. Visitors are surveyed before they are allowed entry and everyone is recorded as they enter and leave the building, which is no bad thing.

Ruth's Story

"I WAS DISCOURAGED FROM HAVING A HOME BIRTH"

Ruth had her second baby, Oliver at home, but was discouraged despite home-births being back in fashion. Here is her story . . .

"I wanted a home-birth for many varied reasons. I didn't want to be away from our other son Edward, who was only two at the time and my first labour had been short, smooth and uncomplicated, so I was concerned that the second labour could be even quicker. I also hoped to have minimal intervention and the thought of giving birth in a familiar place sounded very appealing. I really felt that it was the right thing for all of us.

We had read widely on the subject and dispelled many of the myths associated with a home delivery. For example; that women do not have a right of choice in certain geographical areas and that you must be accepted by a doctor and that it is always safer to have a baby in hospital.

I was however quickly dissuaded from having a home birth at my first antenatal appointment and I reluctantly agreed to a domino delivery. However, at 30 weeks, I began to feel quite strongly that a home birth was what I wanted; yet our decision was met with considerable disapproval by some health professionals. Others however encouraged us along, particularly pro-choice midwives.

I had a trouble free pregnancy that went in favour of my risk assessment and at antenatal class I met a lovely community midwife called Linda, who was happy to deliver my baby at home for me.

At 38 weeks, an appointment confirmed that the baby was well positioned and I should go ahead as planned.

I had a 'show' two weeks before my due date, followed by two more later in the week and spent everyday thinking; 'this will be the day'. With a week to go I had a sudden burst of energy and spent the day shopping with my husband — I knew that it wouldn't be long now.

When I got home, I organised everything and got myself changed into a big pink shirt and rubbed jasmine oil onto my tummy. I kissed my son good night and whispered that he would probably have a baby brother or sister in the morning.

We had arranged for my mother to come and stay and care for Edward during my confinement, but having made herself available all week, that very day I couldn't get hold of her. Eventually, my sister contacted her and she was on her way.

My contractions were now every five minutes and I suddenly had an incredible burning pressure as the baby's head started to show. Our baby Oliver was born on our bed at 11.25pm and twenty minutes later my placenta delivered itself. I felt rather impatient for this to happen and shook uncontrollably for 15 minutes, but I didn't need one stitch!

After a warm bath and returning to find a freshly made bed, the three of us sat and enjoyed tea and biscuits. Edward slept soundly throughout it all!

We reflected on the calmness of the birth and Pete, my husband said that he had felt very deflated when our first son had been delivered because he had been asked to leave the hospital just a few hours after his son had been born. For him, remaining together throughout the first few hours was so important.

I often had reservations during the pregnancy about our decision to go ahead with a home delivery. It would have been much easier to passively agree to a hospital delivery. However, looking back, I have no regrets.

IT WAS TERRIFIC!!"

The Last Word

Well we have come to the end of the book and as we have seen, a lot of changes have taken place over the past fifty years in pregnancy and childbirth.

I am not medically qualified and neither are any of the women who contributed to this book, but all of these stories are real-life stories that have happened to women from all walks of life and from all over the country. It is without their help that this book would still be just a dream and I thank every one of you who helped contribute and let me share your treasured memories of the most important time in your lives.

I thank you all. I wonder just what the next fifty years will hold for our daughters, granddaughters and great-granddaughters experiences? Maybe one of them will continue the story . . .